MATH MADE EASY

3rd Grade Workbook

10 Minutes A Day Math

Author Deborah Lock
Consultant Alison Tribley

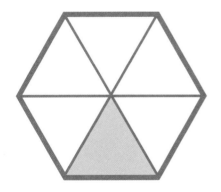

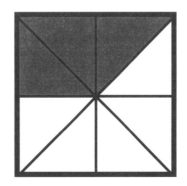

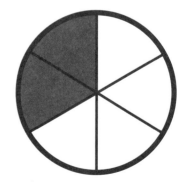

10-minute challenge

Try to complete the exercises for each topic in 10 minutes or less. Note the time it takes you in the "Time taken" column below.

DK London
Editor Elizabeth Blakemore
US Editor Nancy Ellwood
US Math Consultant Alison Tribley
Managing Editor Christine Stroyan
Managing Art Editor Anna Hall
Senior Production Editor Andy Hilliard
Senior Production Controller Jude Crozier
Jacket Design Development Manager Sophia MTT
Publisher Andrew Macintyre
Associate Publishing Director Liz Wheeler
Art Director Karen Self
Publishing Director Jonathan Metcalf

DK Delhi
Senior Editor Rupa Rao
Senior Art Editor Stuti Tiwari Bhatia
Editorial team Dipika Dasgupta, Nayan Keshan, Nishtha Kapil
Assistant Art Editor Tanvi Nathyal
Managing Editors Soma B. Chowdhury, Kingshuk Ghoshal
Managing Art Editor Govind Mittal
Design Consultant Shefali Upadhyay
Senior DTP Designer Tarun Sharma
DTP Designers Anita Yadav, Rakesh Kumar, Harish Aggarwal
Senior Jacket Designer Suhita Dharamjit
Jackets Editorial Coordinator Priyanka Sharma

This American Edition, 2020
First American Edition, 2014
Published in the United States by DK Publishing
1450 Broadway, Suite 801, New York, NY 10018

Copyright © 2014, 2020 Dorling Kindersley Limited
DK, a Division of Penguin Random House LLC
20 21 22 23 24 10 9 8 7 6 5 4 3 2 1
001–322718–May/2020

A catalog record for this book is available from the Library of Congress.
ISBN 978-0-7440-3139-3

DK books are available at special discounts when purchased in bulk for sales promotions, premiums, fund-raising, or educational use.
For details, contact: DK Publishing Special Markets,
1450 Broadway, Suite 801, New York, NY 10018
SpecialSales@dk.com

Printed and bound in Canada

All images © Dorling Kindersley Limited
For further information see: www.dkimages.com

For the curious

www.dk.com

Contents

Time Taken

Time Filler:
In these boxes are some extra challenges to extend your skills. You can do them if you have some time left after finishing the questions. Or these can be stand-alone activities that you can do in 10 minutes.

4

Place Value

How well do you know your numbers?
Let's find out!

(1) Write each number as a word.

42 ....

90 ....

317 ....

(2) How many hundreds are there in each number?

438   560   602

☐   ☐   ☐

(3) What number is this?

☐

Hundreds	Tens	Ones
■		■
■		■ ■
■		■ ■
		■ ■
		■

(4) Write these numbers as digits.

Eighteen   ☐   Two hundred and four   ☐

Sixty-seven   ☐   Five hundred and fifty-two   ☐

Time Filler:
Think of three digits. What is the largest number you can make using all three digits? What is the smallest number you can make with them?

5 What is the largest number you can make with the digits 6, 2, and 8?

What is the smallest number you can make with these same digits?

6 What is 100 more than these numbers?

364

723

900

7 Write these numbers in their expanded forms. For example, 322 can be written as 300 + 20 + 2.

834

674

506

8 Place these numbers onto the place-value grid.

	Thousands	Hundreds	Tens	Ones
350				
536				
1,000				

Telling Time

Here are some time-telling challenges.
How quickly can you do them?
Get ready. Set. Go!

① Circle the clock that says 7:23.

② Draw these times onto the clock faces.

9:30

4:41

11:34

8:06

③ Diego's school lunch break lasts for 45 minutes. Lunch starts at 12:30. What time does it end?

④ Emma is 12 minutes late for her guitar lesson. Her lesson was scheduled to start at 2:50. What time does Emma arrive?

Time Filler:
What time do you wake up? What time do you go to bed? How long are you awake? How many hours do you spend at school?

(5) Check (✔) the earliest time.

 7 : 49 PM

 11 : 26 AM

 5 : 52 PM

(6) What is the date five days after Tuesday, January 28?

....

What is the date eight days before Friday, April 5?

....

(7) Jason's alarm clock is 10 minutes fast. The clock shows 7:43. What is the correct time?

(8) The movie starts at 4:45 PM. The movie lasts 90 minutes. What time did the movie end?

Rounding

A quick way to estimate answers
is to use rounding. Give this a try.

① Round these numbers to the nearest 10.

42   85   679   212

◌◌◌◌◌   ◌◌◌◌◌   ◌◌◌◌◌   ◌◌◌◌◌

② Estimate the total of $58.76 and $32.49 to the nearest $10.

◌◌◌◌◌

③ Round these numbers to the nearest 100.

255   894   428   965

◌◌◌◌◌   ◌◌◌◌◌   ◌◌◌◌◌   ◌◌◌◌◌

④ A television costs $799 and another costs $595.
Estimate the difference in price to the nearest $100.

◌◌◌◌◌

⑤ Round these amounts to the nearest 10 inches.

76 in.   854 in.   649 in.   95 in.

◌◌◌◌◌   ◌◌◌◌◌   ◌◌◌◌◌   ◌◌◌◌◌

Time Filler:
A 1st Grade class has 21 children. A 2nd Grade class has 25 children. A 3rd Grade class has 22 children. What is the estimated number of total children in these 3 classes?

6 Darcy needed 4.75 ft of material to make some curtains. Material was sold in whole feet. How much material did she need?

7 Here is a shopping bill. Estimate the total cost by rounding each item to the nearest 10 cents.

Item	Amount	Rounded to Nearest 10 ¢
Milk	$2.37	
Bread	$2.94	
Carrots	$1.73	
Potatoes	$2.27	
Breakfast Cereal	$3.99	
Dog Food	$2.95	
Eggs	$2.25	
Estimated Total Cost		

8 The school bus leaves after school at 3:13. Round the time to the nearest 10 minutes.

Quadrilaterals

Shapes with four sides are known as quadrilaterals. How many do you know? Let's get started!

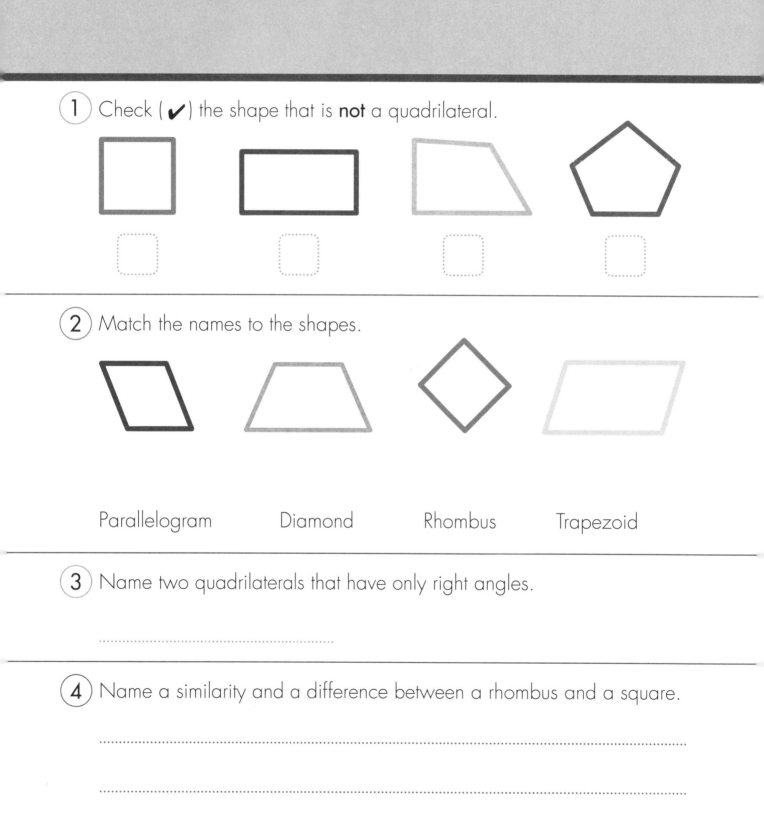

1 Check (✔) the shape that is **not** a quadrilateral.

2 Match the names to the shapes.

Parallelogram   Diamond   Rhombus   Trapezoid

3 Name two quadrilaterals that have only right angles.

....

4 Name a similarity and a difference between a rhombus and a square.

....

....

Time Filler:
Think of a quadrilateral. Can you describe it to a friend without saying its name?
Can your friend name the shape?

5 Mark all the lines of symmetry on these shapes.

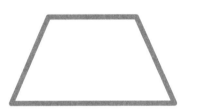  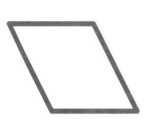

6 Use the metric side of a ruler. Draw a quadrilateral with sides that measure 2 cm, 3 cm, 5 cm, and 4 cm.

7 Check (✔) the quadrilateral that **does not** have any parallel sides.

8 Name this four-sided shape. It has two sets of parallel lines. The opposite sides are equal in length. It has no right angles.

....

Multiplication

Multiplying groups is a quick way
of counting them. Give it a try!

1. A crate has 8 bunches of bananas. Each bunch has 5 bananas.
How many bananas are there in the crate? Fill in the numbers.

   ☐ bunches × ☐ bananas = ☐ bananas

2. Join the questions to the answers with a line.

   3 groups of 4   21

   7 groups of 3   20

   10 groups of 3   12

   5 groups of 4   30

3. How many cookies are there on the tray? Fill in the numbers.

   ☐ rows × ☐ cookies = ☐ cookies

4. Write the answers.

   9 + 9 + 9 + 9 + 9 = ☐   4 groups of 8 = ☐

   5 multiplied by 7 = ☐   6 times 3 = ☐

13

Time Filler:
Can you name three multiples of 5? Can you think of a multiple of both 3 and 4? What is the lowest multiple of 3, 4, and 5?

(5) Fill in the missing numbers in each row.

| 12 | ⬚ | 20 | 24 | ⬚ | ⬚ | ⬚ | 40 |

| 50 | 45 | ⬚ | 35 | ⬚ | ⬚ | ⬚ | 15 |

| 6 | 12 | ⬚ | 24 | ⬚ | ⬚ | 42 | ⬚ |

(6) How many 5 ¢ coins make up 55 ¢?

⬚ coins

(7) A baker makes 3 cakes. He decorates each of them with 9 stars. How many stars does he make? Fill in the numbers.

⬚ cakes × ⬚ stars = ⬚ stars

(8) How many petals are there on each bunch of flowers?

⬚ petals   ⬚ petals   ⬚ petals

Pictographs

Use the picture key to help you work out
the data on the pictograph. How quickly
can you answer the questions?

Look at this graph to see how many loaves of bread a baker
sells in a week.

= 10 loaves   = 5 loaves

Days of the Week	Number of Loaves Sold	Total Sold
Monday		
Tuesday		
Wednesday		
Thursday		
Friday		
Saturday		
Sunday		

1) Fill in the total number of loaves sold for each day.

Time Filler:
Collect data for the number of birds you see in a week. Draw a pictograph for the results. Which type of bird did you see the most? What other information can you find out from your graph?

2 On which day did the baker sell the most loaves?

....

3 How many loaves were sold in total on Monday and Tuesday?

[   ] loaves

4 How many more loaves were sold on Friday than Thursday?

[   ] loaves

5 How many loaves did the baker sell over the weekend?

[   ] loaves

6 How many loaves did the baker sell over the whole week?

[   ] loaves

7 The cost of 5 loaves is $2.50.
How much did the baker make on Tuesday?

[   ]

8 On which day did he make $20 from selling the loaves?

....

Dividing

Group or share equally to divide
these amounts. Be quick.

(1) Share 28 candies equally among 4 children. How many candies
did each child get? Fill in the numbers.

[   ] candies ÷ [   ] children = [   ] candies

(2) Join the questions to the answers with a line.

Divide 20 by 4   9

Divide 45 by 5   12

Divide 77 by 7   5

Divide 36 by 3   11

(3) Sixty children were going on a school trip. They were split into
12 groups. How many children were there in each group?
Fill in the numbers.

[   ] children ÷ [   ] groups = [   ] children

(4) How many groups of 4 are there in

12? [   ]   32? [   ]   48? [   ]

Time Filler:
You have 40 pennies. How many pennies would each person get when shared equally among 5 people, 4 people, or 10 people?

5 Twenty-four cartons of milk are split equally among 3 classes. How many cartons of milk will each class get? Fill in the numbers.

☐ cartons ÷ ☐ classes = ☐ cartons

6 Fill in the missing numbers in each row.

48	40	☐	24	☐	☐	0
63	54	45	☐	☐	18	☐
70	63	☐	49	☐	☐	28

7 A restaurant is set up with 80 chairs split equally around 10 tables. How many chairs are there around each table?

☐ chairs

8 Complete the chart.

×	3	
	18	48
4	12	32

Time Schedules

Practice reading schedules so that you are not late. How much time will it take you to answer the questions?

Look at this schedule for a day at school.

Duration	Activity
8:55–9:05	Morning Announcement
9:05–9:25	Silent Reading
9:25–10:05	Math
10:05–10:45	Social Studies
10:45–11:25	Writing Workshop
11:25–11:50	Lunch
11:50–12:05	Recess
12:05–12:45	Spelling
12:45–1:25	Gym
1:25–2:05	Science
2:05–2:25	Snack
2:25–3:05	Art

1. What time did the school day begin?

2. How long was Math?

3. How much longer was snacktime than recess?

Time Filler:
Think about your schedule for today.
Where will you be at 11:00? What
will you be doing at 3:00?

(4) What was the class doing at 10:30?

....

(5) How long was Spelling?

(6) Which activity was the same length as Silent Reading?

....

(7) What was the class doing at 1:30?

....

(8) If the school bus left 10 minutes after the last activity
finished, what time did the bus leave?

SCHOOL BUS

XYZ 123

20

Beat the Clock 1

Can you recall your times tables quickly?

1) 10 x 10 = ☐   2) 10 x 8 = ☐   3) 2 x 7 = ☐

4) 2 x 2 = ☐   5) 10 x 0 = ☐   6) 5 x 6 = ☐

7) 3 x 3 = ☐   8) 10 x 9 = ☐   9) 4 x 3 = ☐

10) 4 x 4 = ☐   11) 12 x 2 = ☐   12) 7 x 1 = ☐

13) 5 x 5 = ☐   14) 11 x 2 = ☐   15) 2 x 3 = ☐

16) 6 x 6 = ☐   17) 11 x 4 = ☐   18) 4 x 5 = ☐

19) 7 x 7 = ☐   20) 12 x 5 = ☐   21) 4 x 8 = ☐

22) 8 x 8 = ☐   23) 2 x 6 = ☐   24) 3 x 6 = ☐

25) 9 x 9 = ☐   26) 10 x 5 = ☐   27) 9 x 2 = ☐

28) 4 x 0 = ☐   29) 11 x 3 = ☐   30) 9 x 1 = ☐

Time Filler:
Check your answers on page 80. Return
to this page again to improve your score.

(31) $4 \times 7 = $ [ ]

(32) $4 \times 6 = $ [ ]

(33) $10 \times 6 = $ [ ]

(34) $3 \times 4 = $ [ ]

(35) $9 \times 3 = $ [ ]

(36) $12 \times 4 = $ [ ]

(37) $9 \times 8 = $ [ ]

(38) $6 \times 7 = $ [ ]

(39) $10 \times 7 = $ [ ]

(40) $5 \times 0 = $ [ ]

(41) $2 \times 9 = $ [ ]

(42) $11 \times 5 = $ [ ]

(43) $9 \times 4 = $ [ ]

(44) $6 \times 8 = $ [ ]

(45) $11 \times 6 = $ [ ]

(46) $5 \times 7 = $ [ ]

(47) $2 \times 4 = $ [ ]

(48) $10 \times 3 = $ [ ]

(49) $5 \times 1 = $ [ ]

(50) $3 \times 5 = $ [ ]

(51) $5 \times 9 = $ [ ]

(52) $3 \times 9 = $ [ ]

(53) $5 \times 8 = $ [ ]

(54) $10 \times 4 = $ [ ]

(55) $2 \times 8 = $ [ ]

(56) $3 \times 7 = $ [ ]

(57) $12 \times 6 = $ [ ]

(58) $3 \times 8 = $ [ ]

(59) $9 \times 5 = $ [ ]

(60) $12 \times 3 = $ [ ]

Multiplying Fun

Try out some tricks to solve multiplication problems. Give it a try!

1 Complete this number sentence.

If $8 \times 4 = 32$, then $4 \times 8 = $ ☐

2 Try these number sentences.

If $9 \times 3 = 27$, then $3 \times 9 = $ ☐

If $6 \times 8 = 48$, then $8 \times 6 = $ ☐

3 Fill in the missing numbers.
What is $3 \times 4 \times 2$?

$3 \times 4 = $ ☐ then $12 \times 2 = $ ☐

4 Find the answers.

$2 \times 5 \times 3 = $ ☐ $4 \times 4 \times 1 = $ ☐ $3 \times 10 \times 3 = $ ☐

5 Some times tables are hard to learn, but there are tricks to use!
Fill in the missing numbers.
What is 8×7?

$8 \times (5 + $ ☐ $) = (8 \times 5) + ($ ☐ $\times 2) = 40 + $ ☐ $= $ ☐

Time Filler:
Does the bracket method help you? Try
out 6 x 12 and 4 x 14 using this method.

(6) Fill in the missing numbers.

6 x 9 = 6 x (4 + ⬚) = (6 x 4) + (⬚ x 5) = ⬚ + ⬚ = 54

4 x 12 = 4 x (10 + ⬚) = (4 x ⬚) + (⬚ x 2) = ⬚ + 8 = ⬚

(7) Fill in the numbers.

×	6	7	8	9
2	12			
3				
4			32	
5				

(8) What is 25 ¢ multiplied by 4?

⬚

Tiling Areas

What amount of space are these shapes taking up? On your mark. Get set. Go!

1 Count the square tiles to find the area of each shape.

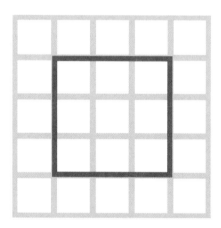

Area = ⬚ squares

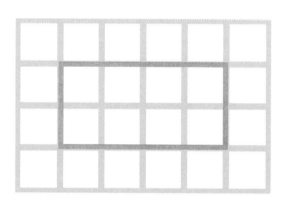

Area = ⬚ squares

Area = ⬚ squares

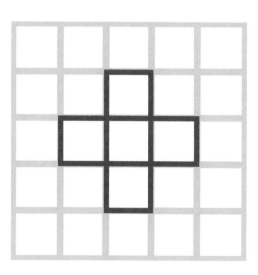

Area = ⬚ squares

Time Filler:
Use some graph paper. How many different rectangles can you draw with an area of 24 squares?

② Use a ruler to draw these shapes.

Draw a square with an area of 16 squares.

Draw a rectangle with an area of 15 squares.

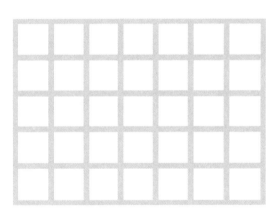

Draw a rectangle with an area of 20 squares.

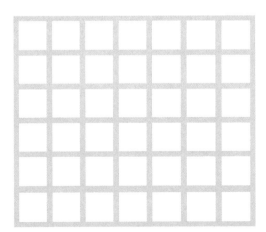

Draw any shape with an area of 14 squares.

26

Patterns

Can you spot the rule in each of these patterns? See how quickly you can work them out!

(1) Circle the odd numbers in this pattern.

3   6   9   12   15   18   21

(2) Complete this pattern.

4   8   12   ☐   ☐   ☐

Are the answers odd or even?   ....

(3) Fill in the missing numbers.

(+3)   45   ☐   ☐   ☐   ☐   60

(−3)   81   ☐   ☐   ☐   ☐   66

(4) What is happening in these patterns?

30   36   42   48   54   60   ....

80   72   64   56   48   40   ....

Time Filler:
On a 1–100 grid, color all the multiples of 6 and 8. What pattern do you see? Are any multiples in both colors?

5) This grid has numbers from 1 to 100.

1	2	3	4	5	6	7	8	9	10
11	12	13	14	15	16	17	18	19	20
21	22	23	24	25	26	27	28	29	30
31	32	33	34	35	36	37	38	39	40
41	42	43	44	45	46	47	48	49	50
51	52	53	54	55	56	57	58	59	60
61	62	63	64	65	66	67	68	69	70
71	72	73	74	75	76	77	78	79	80
81	82	83	84	85	86	87	88	89	90
91	92	93	94	95	96	97	98	99	100

Color all the multiples of 3 red.

Color all the multiples of 4 green.

Color all the multiples of 5 blue.

Which numbers are multiples of 3 and 5?

Which number is a multiple of 3, 4, and 5?

Volume of Liquids

Try these liquid-volume challenges using US Customary System and metric units of measurements. Feeling confident?

1. If 2 cups = 1 pint, and 2 pints = 1 quart, how many cups are there in 1 quart?

2. Carol bought 10 pints of juice. How many cups does this make?
Note: 2 cups = 1 pint.

3. Twenty-four children each drank half a cup of milk at school. How many whole cups of milk did they drink?

4. If 1 gallon = 8 pints, how many pints are there in a 4-gallon barrel that is full?

5. How many milliliters are there in a 1-liter bottle of water?

Time Filler:
If you had 3 gallons of milk, how many quart-size measuring cups could you fill? Remember: 1 gallon = 8 pints, and 2 pints = 1 quart.

---

(6) How much water is there in the measuring cup? Measure in milliliters.

---

(7) Round these volumes to the nearest 10 ml.

65 ml

346 ml

673 ml

---

(8) Six children each drank 8 ml of juice. How much juice did they drink in total? Mark this on the measuring cup.

Adding

Keep your adding skills in good shape
with these problems. Are you ready
to test your knowledge? Go!

① Complete the problems.

$6 + 8 + 4 =$ ☐

$16 + 18 + 14 =$ ☐

② Janet bought 2 pencils and a notepad. What was the total cost?

☐

③ Solve these problems.

42	63	24	76
		17	53
+29	+37	+25	+49
....	....	....	....

④ Add these amounts.

$\$3.00 + 84¢ + \$1.95 =$ ☐

$357\,ml + 69\,ml + 283\,ml =$ ☐

Time Filler:
Create three 2-digit numbers using the digits 4, 6, and 7. What is the total of the numbers? Can you change one of the numbers to make the total larger?

(5) On a vacation, a family drove 213 miles from New York City to Boston, then 440 miles to Washington, D.C. Then they drove 229 miles back to New York City. How far did they drive?

(6) Three runners raised the following amounts in a charity run. How much did they give to the charity altogether?

Runner 1: $167.50
Runner 2: $252.95
Runner 3: $172.29

(7) Solve these problems.

```
  254        528        257        402
+393       +432        154        365
                      +321       + 42
```

(8) Look at the chart below. What is the total money Mom spent shopping?

Item	Price
Skirt	$ 89.75
Coat	$126.00
Shoes	$ 65.49
Hat	$ 54.32
Shirt	$ 36.99
Total	

Bar Graphs

These graphs present data in a block or bar.
Good luck, and have some fun!

1 A pet food company asked children to vote for their favorite pets.
The picture graph shows the results. Each picture is for 5 votes.

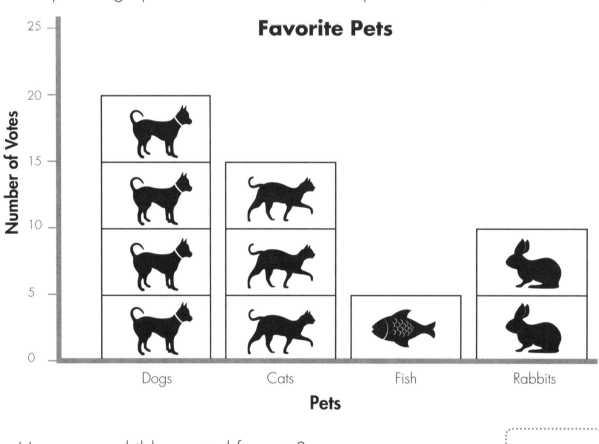

Favorite Pets

How many children voted for cats?

What was the children's favorite pet?

How many children voted?

How many more children voted for cats than fish?

Time Filler:
Collect data about the favorite foods of your friends and family. Draw a bar graph to show the data.

② 100 children were asked to vote for their favorite ice cream flavors. The bar graph shows the results.

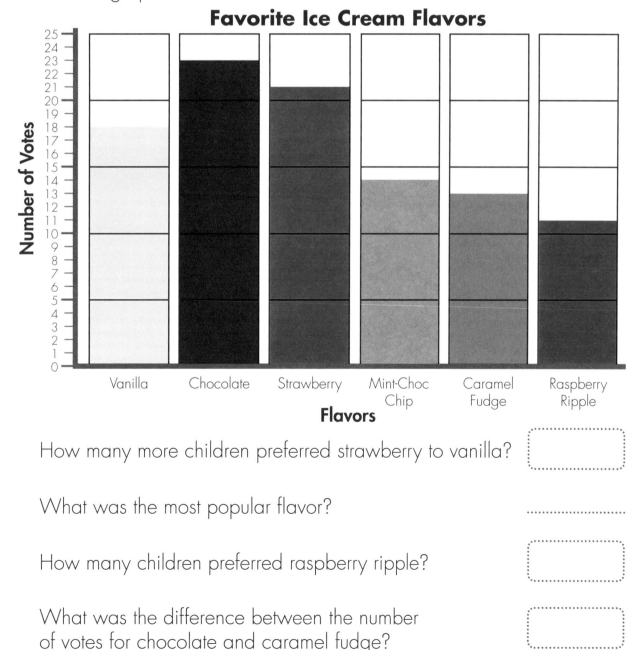

Favorite Ice Cream Flavors

How many more children preferred strawberry to vanilla?

What was the most popular flavor?

How many children preferred raspberry ripple?

What was the difference between the number of votes for chocolate and caramel fudge?

34

Subtracting

How good are your subtracting skills?

① Complete these problems.

83 – 19 = ☐

56 – 34 = ☐

② Jake saved $265.49, and Mike saved $386.25.
How much more did Mike save than Jake?

☐

③ Solve these problems.

74	130	462	538
– 46	– 28	– 354	– 219

④ Subtract these amounts.

$3.00 – 84 ¢ = ☐

357 ml – 69 ml = ☐

Time Filler:
Create two 3-digit numbers using the digits 2, 8, and 9. Take away the smaller number from the larger one. What is your answer?

---

(5) The distance between Miami and New Orleans is 892 miles. Dallas is only 504 miles from New Orleans. By how many miles is Dallas closer to New Orleans than Miami?

---

(6) Subtract these amounts.

800	513	693	795
− 248	− 270	− 281	− 426

---

(7) How much did this television set cost in the sale?

SALE $150 off

$853.99

---

(8) Dad spent $37.64 shopping. He paid $50. How much change did he get?

Perimeters

Add the length of each side to find the
perimeter around each shape. Are you
sitting comfortably? Then start.

(1) Find the perimeters of each of these shapes.

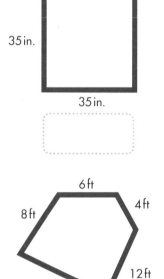

35 in.

35 in.

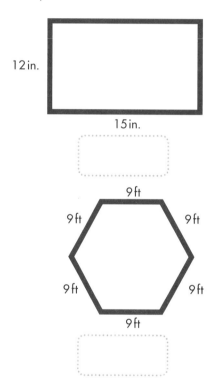

12 in.

15 in.

6 ft

8 ft

4 ft

12 ft

15 ft

9 ft

9 ft

9 ft

9 ft

9 ft

9 ft

(2) Draw a rectangle with a perimeter of 10 inches. Use a ruler.

Time Filler:
Measure the sides of a rectangular table top.
What is the perimeter of the table top?

(3) Write the measurements that are missing.

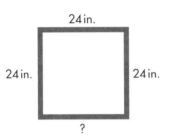

Perimeter = 96 in.

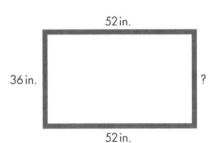

Perimeter = 176 in.

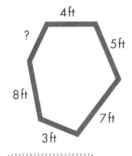

Perimeter = 30 ft

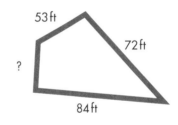

Perimeter = 250 ft

(4) Draw a regular pentagon with a perimeter of 5 inches. Use a ruler.

38

Solving Problems

Read each problem carefully. Choose whether to add, subtract, multiply, or divide. Are you ready? Then go!

1 Sasha receives $2.15 change after giving the shopkeeper $5.

How much did Sasha spend?

....

2 Chris wants to buy a toy that costs $9.99. He has $5.70.

How much more does Chris need to buy the toy?

....

3 On his birthday, Otto was given $15 by his Grandma, $10 by his uncle, and $5 by his aunt.

How much money did Otto receive in total?

....

4 A builder buys three lengths of wood, each of which is 9 ft long. He only needs 25 ft total.

What length of wood does the builder need to cut off the third piece of wood?

....

Time Filler:
60 children and 12 adults are going on a school trip. Two school buses are used, and each bus has 44 seats. How many seats will remain unoccupied?

(5) A businessman flew 242 miles from Houston to Dallas and back again.

What is the total distance he traveled?

(6) Jasmine's watch is 20 minutes slow. The watch shows the time as 3:45.

What time should the watch show?

(7) Kate fills a glass with 125 ml of juice and then adds 250 ml of water.

How much liquid is in the glass?

(8) Two adults and three children went to a fair. The tickets cost $3.50 each for an adult and $2.50 each for a child.

How much did the tickets cost altogether?

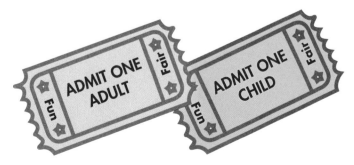

Beat the Clock 2

Try out these quick add and subtract questions. There are 60 questions—that is 10 seconds for each one. Get set. Go!

(1) $12 + 9 =$

(2) $16 + 9 =$

(3) $3 + 7 + 5 =$

(4) $13 + 7 =$

(5) $14 + 19 =$

(6) $7 + 8 + 2 =$

(7) $22 + 9 =$

(8) $18 + 6 =$

(9) $9 + 3 + 7 =$

(10) $23 + 14 =$

(11) $16 + 17 =$

(12) $1 + 8 + 4 =$

(13) $21 + 8 =$

(14) $15 + 12 =$

(15) $4 + 3 + 9 =$

(16) $53 + 22 =$

(17) $30 + 26 =$

(18) $6 + 6 + 7 =$

(19) $48 + 32 =$

(20) $29 + 17 =$

(21) $2 + 6 + 4 =$

(22) $23 + 49 =$

(23) $19 + 19 =$

(24) $5 + 5 + 9 =$

(25) $54 + 28 =$

(26) $36 + 10 =$

(27) $1 + 9 + 6 =$

(28) $55 + 63 =$

(29) $34 + 29 =$

(30) $7 + 2 + 5 =$

Time Filler:
Check your answers on page 80. Return to this page again to improve your score.

31) $16 - 9 =$ [ ] 32) $45 - 8 =$ [ ] 33) $100 - 28 =$ [ ]

34) $11 - 8 =$ [ ] 35) $47 - 9 =$ [ ] 36) $42 - 16 =$ [ ]

37) $15 - 7 =$ [ ] 38) $95 - 9 =$ [ ] 39) $66 - 29 =$ [ ]

40) $55 - 9 =$ [ ] 41) $62 - 6 =$ [ ] 42) $25 - 17 =$ [ ]

43) $13 - 9 =$ [ ] 44) $26 - 8 =$ [ ] 45) $91 - 18 =$ [ ]

46) $12 - 3 =$ [ ] 47) $32 - 7 =$ [ ] 48) $34 - 16 =$ [ ]

49) $22 - 3 =$ [ ] 50) $35 - 8 =$ [ ] 51) $48 - 15 =$ [ ]

52) $11 - 6 =$ [ ] 53) $28 - 9 =$ [ ] 54) $73 - 11 =$ [ ]

55) $31 - 6 =$ [ ] 56) $29 - 8 =$ [ ] 57) $84 - 15 =$ [ ]

58) $16 - 8 =$ [ ] 59) $47 - 10 =$ [ ] 60) $100 - 34 =$ [ ]

Multiples of 10

Increase or decrease numbers in groups
of 10. How quickly can you zoom
through these questions?

(1) Complete the sequence.

0   10   20   [ ] [ ] [ ] [ ] [ ] [ ] [ ]   100

(2) Write the answers.

$4 \times 30 =$ [ ] $2 \times 40 =$ [ ] $3 \times 50 =$ [ ]

(3) Forty children went on a theater trip. The cost of the bus was $3
for each child. The cost of the tickets was $6 for each child.

What was the total cost of the bus?   [ ]

What was the total cost of the tickets?   [ ]

What was the total cost of the trip?   [ ]

(4) How many minutes are there in 4 hours?

[ ]

Time Filler:
Can you calculate 10 x 10?
What is 10 x 10 x 10?

(5) Write the answers.

60	70	30
x 5	x 4	x 8

....

(6) A box of cookies contains 8 packets.
Each packet contains 20 cookies.
How many cookies are there
in the box?

.... cookies

(7) A square garden plot is marked out with sides that are 20 ft each.
What is the perimeter of the plot?

(8) A DVD stack has 8 rows and can hold 400 DVDs. Each row can fit
an equal number of DVDs. How many DVDs can fit on each row?

.... DVDs

Measuring Weight

Try these challenges about the weights
of fruit. Let's get going!

1 Read these measuring scales. Record the weights of the fruit
on the chart below. Then answer the questions on page 45
using the data below.

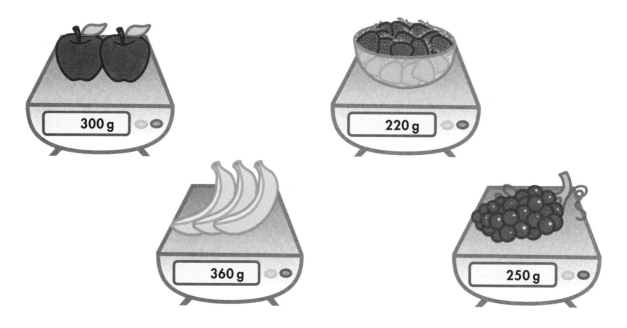

Item	Weight (grams)
2 apples	
3 bananas	
Grapes	
Strawberries	

Time Filler:
Choose 5 objects. Estimate each of their weights before weighing them. How close were your estimates to the actual weights?

(2) What is the estimated weight of 1 apple?

(3) What is the estimated weight of 1 banana?

(4) What is the total weight of the fruit?

(5) What is the difference between the weight of the grapes and the weight of the strawberries?

(6) What will be the weight of 2 bunches of grapes?

(7) What is half the weight of the strawberries?

(8) If you share the grapes equally among 5 friends, what is the weight of the grapes that each person will get?

Equations

Can you find the missing numbers
to replace the letters?

① What number is a?

$2 + a = 5$ ☐

$a - 6 = 10$ ☐

$4 + a = 11$ ☐

$8 - a = 3$ ☐

$a \times 10 = 120$ ☐

$a \div 6 = 5$ ☐

② Josh thinks of a number, takes 4 away from it, and adds 7.
The answer is 13. What is the number Josh started with?

☐

③ I am four times bigger than 40.
What number am I?

☐

④ What number is b?

$14 + 6 = 25 - b$ ☐

$12 - 3 = 5 + b$ ☐

$36 \div 4 = 3 \times b$ ☐

$2 \times 6 = 12 \times b$ ☐

Time Filler:
Write your own number riddle questions and then test them out on a friend.

(5) Figure out each number on these teddy bears.

Double me to make 24.

Take away 37 from 70 to get me.

Add 3 to me to make 15.

Subtract 19 from me to make 5.

Multiply me by 6 to get 54.

Divide me by 4 to get 7.

Line Graph

A line graph shows how some data changes.
How quickly can you complete this page?

A poodle puppy was weighed once a week.
The data below shows the weight for the first ten weeks.

Week	0	1	2	3	4	5	6	7	8	9	10
Weight (in Ounces)	3	5	7	8	$9\frac{1}{2}$	11	$12\frac{1}{2}$	$14\frac{1}{2}$	16	$17\frac{1}{2}$	19

Plot the data on the line graph.

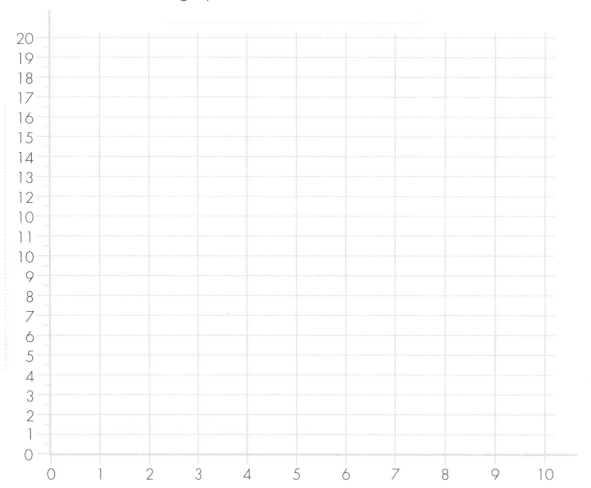

1. Give the line graph a title and label the x-axis and the y-axis.

2. What was the puppy's weight when it was born?

3. How much did the puppy grow in the first week?

4. In which week did the puppy weigh 8 oz.?

5. What is the difference between the puppy's weights from Week 5 to Week 10?

6. How much heavier was the puppy in Week 7 than in Week 4?

7. Between which two weeks did the puppy grow one ounce?

8. How much did the puppy grow in weight over the 10 weeks?

Fractions of a Whole

Try out these fraction challenges. Will you get the whole page right?

(1) Place these fractions on the number line:

$$\frac{1}{2} \quad \frac{1}{4} \quad \frac{3}{4} \quad \frac{1}{3} \quad \frac{2}{3}$$

0   1

(2) Divide this pizza into 4 equal parts.

(3) Split this cake into 8 equal slices.

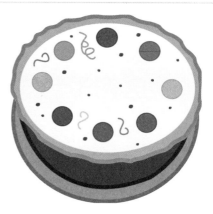

(4) Cut this breadstick into 3 equal parts.

Time Filler:
If an apple is divided into 3 parts, and
2 parts are eaten, what fraction is left?

⑤ How many equal parts has
this pizza been cut into?

⑥ Write the fraction for

a half,   a quarter,   a third,   three quarters.

⑦ An orange has 12 segments.
How many segments are there
in a quarter of the orange?

⑧ How much of the cake has not been eaten?

Fractions of Shapes

Have a try at finding and making
fractions of shapes. How quickly
can you find the answers?

① Color in the fractions on these shapes.

Color in half ($\frac{1}{2}$).   Color in three quarters ($\frac{3}{4}$).   Color in a quarter ($\frac{1}{4}$).

Color in a fifth ($\frac{1}{5}$).   Color in a third ($\frac{1}{3}$).   Color in a sixth ($\frac{1}{6}$).

② Circle the shape which is half colored.

Time Filler:
Which fraction is bigger: $\frac{1}{4}$ of a circle or $\frac{1}{2}$ of a circle? Draw a square. How many ways can this be split in half?

3 Count the number of equal parts.

 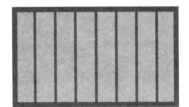 

4 Complete the fractions. Count how many equal parts have been colored.

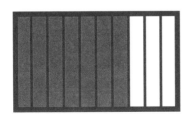  

$\overline{10}$ $\qquad$ $\overline{8}$ $\qquad$ $\overline{5}$

Compare Fractions

Look carefully at the denominator and
numerator to solve these problems.

(1) Compare these fractions. Use the symbols > (greater than)
or < (less than).

$\frac{2}{5}$ ☐ $\frac{4}{5}$ $\frac{6}{7}$ ☐ $\frac{3}{7}$ $\frac{7}{10}$ ☐ $\frac{4}{10}$

$\frac{1}{4}$ ☐ $\frac{3}{4}$ $\frac{5}{8}$ ☐ $\frac{3}{8}$ $\frac{2}{3}$ ☐ $\frac{3}{3}$

(2) Write a larger fraction with the same denominator.

$\frac{1}{4}$ < ☐ $\frac{3}{5}$ < ☐

$\frac{1}{8}$ < ☐ $\frac{6}{10}$ < ☐

(3) Write a smaller fraction with the same denominator.

$\frac{4}{5}$ > ☐ $\frac{4}{6}$ > ☐

$\frac{5}{8}$ > ☐ $\frac{9}{12}$ > ☐

Time Filler:
A pizza was split into 8 equal slices. Ellie ate 3 slices, and Dan ate $\frac{5}{8}$ of the pizza. Who ate more slices?

4 Color a larger fraction of each of these shapes.

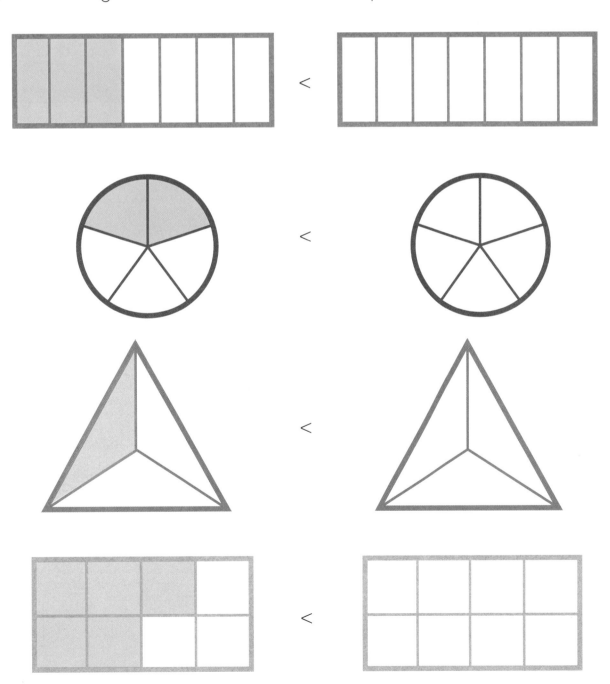

Measuring Problems

Read each problem carefully. Choose whether to add, subtract, multiply, or divide. Get ready. Get set. Go!

(1) A bag of candy weighs 50 grams. What is the weight of 9 bags?

....

(2) A length of wood is 4 ft. What will be the length of 7 pieces of wood?

....

(3) A pound of apples costs $3. How much will 6 pounds of apples cost?

....

(4) How many hours are there in 2 days?

....

Time Filler:
A brick weighs 5 lbs. How heavy are 20 bricks? How many bricks weigh 50 lbs altogether?

5 A car travels at a speed of 30 mph.
How far will the car travel in half an hour?

6 A family-sized bag has 10 small bags of potato chips inside.
Each small bag weighs 20 grams. What is the weight of the family-sized bag?

7 What is the perimeter of this garden?

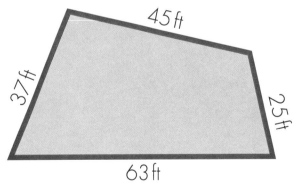

45 ft

37 ft

25 ft

63 ft

8 The time in New York City is 11:42 AM.
What is the time in San Francisco, which is three hours behind?

Equivalent Fractions

Can you work out the fractions that
are the same amount? Are you ready
for the challenge?

(1) Color a fraction of the same amount on these shapes.
Write the fraction.

$$\frac{2}{4} =$$

$$\frac{4}{10} =$$

$$\frac{2}{8} =$$

$$\frac{2}{6} =$$

$$\frac{6}{8} =$$

$$\frac{8}{10} =$$

Time Filler:
How many fractions equivalent to $\frac{2}{5}$ can you find? Remember: Multiply the numerator and denominator by the same amount.

(2) If 1 whole pizza is written as the fraction $\frac{1}{1}$ and 2 whole pizzas is written as the fraction $\frac{2}{1}$, what is the fraction for 3 whole pizzas?

(3) Fill in the numerators to complete these fractions.

$$\frac{\square}{4} = 1 \qquad \frac{\square}{3} = 1 \qquad \frac{\square}{8} = 1 \qquad \frac{\square}{2} = 2$$

(4) Color a fraction of the same amount on these circles.
Write the mixed fraction.

   =

$$2\frac{2}{6} \qquad\qquad = \qquad \square \frac{\square}{\square}$$

Areas

How much space or area do these arrays and 2-D shapes cover?

① What is the area of these arrays?

4 rows of 3 = ⬚

4 rows of 6 = ⬚

1 row of 12 = ⬚

3 rows of 5 = ⬚

3 rows of 4 = ⬚

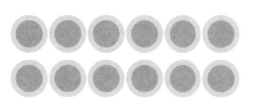

2 rows of 6 = ⬚

4 rows of 4 = ⬚

Time Filler:
Use some paper with squares. How many different shapes can you draw in an area of 12 squares?

(2) Find the areas of the square and the rectangle.

Remember: Multiply the length and the width to find the area.

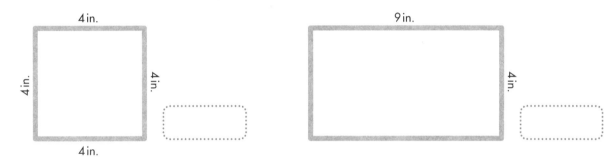

(3) Find the areas of these shapes.
Remember: Split the shape into rectangles then find the area of each rectangle. Add the areas together to find the total area.

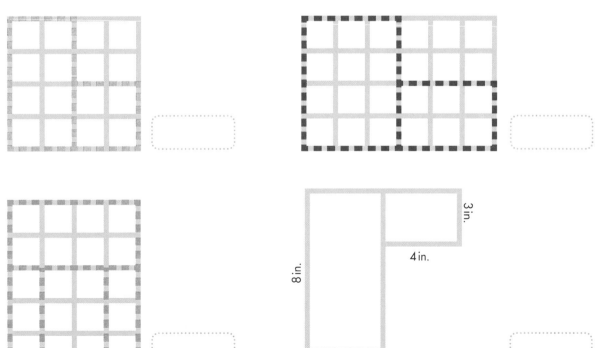

More Problems

Here are some number challenges
to keep your skills in top shape.

1. There are 20 trees in each row. There are 8 rows.
How many trees are there altogether?

   trees

2. A farmer has 72 brown cows and 228 black cows.

   How many more black cows
   are there than brown cows?

   cows

3. Ann bought 4 DVDs that cost $2.85,
$3.74, $2.94, and $4.35.

   What was the total cost?

4. One book costs 80 ¢.
How much will 6 books cost?

Time Filler:
Look at the back of this book to find the price. How much would 3 of these books cost?

(5) Jim bought a present that cost $3.59.

How much change did he get from a $5 bill?

(6) Forty children went on a school trip.
They were split into 5 equal groups.

How many children were there in each group? children

(7) Dad cut a large pizza into 8 slices and gave an equal amount to each of his 4 children.

How many slices did each child get? slices

(8) Mom baked 12 cupcakes. She decorated half with blue icing, a quarter with yellow icing, and the rest with red icing.

How many cupcakes had red icing? cupcakes

Beat the Clock 3

Try out these questions to test
your mental arithmetic skills.

(1) $7 + 8 = \boxed{}$ (2) $406 - 285 = \boxed{}$ (3) $\boxed{} + 8 = 16$

(4) $8 + 4 = \boxed{}$ (5) $136 + 108 = \boxed{}$ (6) $\boxed{} \times 9 = 45$

(7) $9 + 5 = \boxed{}$ (8) $240 - 37 = \boxed{}$ (9) $\boxed{} \times 5 = 0$

(10) $7 + 6 = \boxed{}$ (11) $560 - 29 = \boxed{}$ (12) $\boxed{} + 7 = 25$

(13) $9 + 9 = \boxed{}$ (14) $826 - 314 = \boxed{}$ (15) $\boxed{} + 9 = 30$

(16) $16 - 7 = \boxed{}$ (17) $346 - 225 = \boxed{}$ (18) $\boxed{} \div 3 = 7$

(19) $14 - 8 = \boxed{}$ (20) $7 + 6 + 3 = \boxed{}$ (21) $\boxed{} \div 2 = 12$

(22) $15 - 9 = \boxed{}$ (23) $17 + 16 + 13 = \boxed{}$ (24) $\boxed{} - 6 = 30$

(25) $12 - 7 = \boxed{}$ (26) $36 + 24 + 10 = \boxed{}$ (27) $\boxed{} - 14 = 6$

(28) $13 - 5 = \boxed{}$ (29) $22 + 24 + 26 = \boxed{}$ (30) $\boxed{} \times 4 = 32$

Time Filler:
Check your answers on page 80. Return to this page again to improve your score.

(31) $31 + 7 =$ [ ]

(32) $13 + $ [ ] $= 20$

(33) $9 \times 3 =$ [ ]

(34) $35 + 14 =$ [ ]

(35) $18 + $ [ ] $= 24$

(36) $6 \times 5 =$ [ ]

(37) $52 + 20 =$ [ ]

(38) $13 - $ [ ] $= 9$

(39) $7 \times 4 =$ [ ]

(40) $17 + 23 =$ [ ]

(41) $22 - $ [ ] $= 14$

(42) $20 \times 3 =$ [ ]

(43) $29 + 61 =$ [ ]

(44) $40 \div $ [ ] $= 8$

(45) $40 \times 2 =$ [ ]

(46) $58 - 23 =$ [ ]

(47) $35 \div $ [ ] $= 5$

(48) $18 \div 3 =$ [ ]

(49) $96 - 64 =$ [ ]

(50) $48 \div $ [ ] $= 12$

(51) $16 \div 4 =$ [ ]

(52) $72 - 40 =$ [ ]

(53) $33 - $ [ ] $= 25$

(54) $50 \div 10 =$ [ ]

(55) $80 - 42 =$ [ ]

(56) $5 \times $ [ ] $= 30$

(57) $48 \div 4 =$ [ ]

(58) $55 - 26 =$ [ ]

(59) $3 \times $ [ ] $= 27$

(60) $60 \div 3 =$ [ ]

66

Answers:

4–5 Place Value
6–7 Telling Time

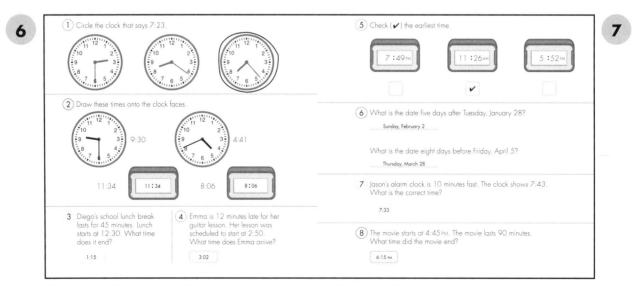

4

① Write each number as a word.

42 _____ forty-two

90 _____ ninety

317 _____ three hundred and seventeen

② How many hundreds are there in each number?

438   560   602

4   5   6

③ What number is this?

309

Hundreds	Tens	Ones
■ ■ ■		■ ■ ■ ■ ■ ■ ■ ■ ■

4 Write these numbers as digits.

Eighteen   18   Two hundred and four   204

Sixty-seven   67   Five hundred and fifty-two   552

5

⑤ What is the largest number you can make with the digits 6, 2, and 8?

862

What is the smallest number you can make with these same digits?

268

⑥ What is 100 more than these numbers?

364   723   900

464   823   1,000

⑦ Write these numbers in their expanded forms. For example, 322 can be written as 300 + 20 + 2.

834   800 + 30 + 4   674   600 + 70 + 4

506   500 + 6

⑧ Place these numbers onto the place-value grid.

	Thousands	Hundreds	Tens	Ones
350		3	5	0
536		5	3	6
1,000	1	0	0	0

Children at this age understand multi-digit whole numbers in terms of hundreds, tens, and ones. These activities help to reinforce the place value of numbers, and how the digits can be understood in their expanded form. This knowledge will help them understand and perform multi-digit arithmetic.

6

① Circle the clock that says 7:23.

② Draw these times onto the clock faces.

9:30   4:41

11:34   11:34   8:06   8:06

3 Diego's school lunch break lasts for 45 minutes. Lunch starts at 12:30. What time does it end?

1:15

④ Emma is 12 minutes late for her guitar lesson. Her lesson was scheduled to start at 2:50. What time does Emma arrive?

3:02

7

⑤ Check (✔) the earliest time.

7:49 PM   11:26 AM   5:52 PM

✔

⑥ What is the date five days after Tuesday, January 28?

Sunday, February 2

What is the date eight days before Friday, April 5?

Thursday, March 28

7 Jason's alarm clock is 10 minutes fast. The clock shows 7:43. What is the correct time?

7:33

⑧ The movie starts at 4:45 PM. The movie lasts 90 minutes. What time did the movie end?

6:15 PM

Children should be able to tell and write times to the nearest minute and measure time intervals in minutes. The word problems need to be solved using addition and subtraction of time intervals. If your child needs support, encourage her/him to either represent the problem on a number line or use an actual clock.

Answers:

8-9 Rounding
10-11 Quadrilaterals

8

1) Round these numbers to the nearest 10.

42	85	679	212
40	90	680	210

2) Estimate the total of $58.76 and $32.49 to the nearest $10.

$90

3) Round these numbers to the nearest 100.

255	894	428	965
300	900	400	1,000

4) A television costs $799 and another costs $595. Estimate the difference in price to the nearest $100.

$200

5) Round these amounts to the nearest 10 inches.

76 in.	854 in.	649 in.	95 in.
80 in.	850 in.	650 in.	100 in.

9

6) Darcy needed 4.75 ft of material to make some curtains. Material was sold in whole feet. How much material did she need?

5 ft

7) Here is a shopping bill. Estimate the total cost by rounding each item to the nearest 10 cents.

Item	Amount	Rounded to Nearest 10¢
Milk	$2.37	$2.40
Bread	$2.94	$2.90
Carrots	$1.73	$1.70
Potatoes	$2.27	$2.30
Breakfast Cereal	$3.99	$4.00
Dog Food	$2.95	$3.00
Eggs	$2.25	$2.30
Estimated Total Cost		$18.60

8) The school bus leaves after school at 3:13. Round the time to the nearest 10 minutes.

3:10

Good understanding of place value will help children round numbers to the nearest 10 or 100. Children should identify the ones digit to round to the nearest 10, and the tens digit to round to the nearest 100. Here is a fun way to remember the rounding rules: "Five or more raise the score. Four or less let it rest." Rounding is useful for estimating amounts for multi-digit arithmetic.

10

1) Check (✔) the shape that is **not** a quadrilateral.

2) Match the names to the shapes.
Parallelogram   Diamond   Rhombus   Trapezoid

3) Name two quadrilaterals that have only right angles.

Square and rectangle

4) Name a similarity and a difference between a rhombus and a square.

Similarity—All sides are the same length or there are two sets of parallel lines.

Difference—All corners of a square are right angles.

11

5) Mark all the lines of symmetry on these shapes.

6) Use the metric side of a ruler. Draw a quadrilateral with sides that measure 2 cm, 3 cm, 5 cm, and 4 cm.

7) Check (✔) the quadrilateral that **does not** have any parallel sides.

8) Name this four-sided shape. It has two sets of parallel lines. The opposite sides are equal in length. It has no right angles.

Parallelogram

Working with quadrilateral shapes helps to understand that some shapes share similar features that define them in a larger category. Children should be able to recognize named quadrilaterals such as rhombus or square, but they should also be able to identify all four-sided figures as quadrilaterals. As they begin the higher grade levels, they will be able to determine if quadrilaterals are regular or irregular.

Answers:

12-13 Multiplication
14-15 Pictographs

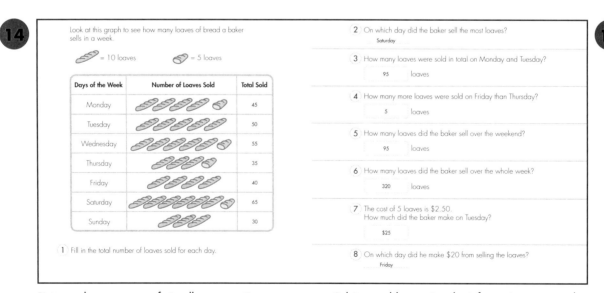

12

1) A crate has 8 bunches of bananas. Each bunch has 5 bananas. How many bananas are there in the crate? Fill in the numbers.

8 bunches × 5 bananas = 40 bananas

2) Join the questions to the answers with a line.

3 groups of 4 — 21
7 groups of 3 — 20
10 groups of 3 — 12
5 groups of 4 — 30

3) How many cookies are there on the tray? Fill in the numbers.

6 rows × 5 cookies = 30 cookies

4) Write the answers.

9 + 9 + 9 + 9 + 9 = 45   4 groups of 8 = 32

5 multiplied by 7 = 35   6 times 3 = 18

13

5) Fill in the missing numbers in each row.

12 16 20 24 28 32 36 40

50 45 40 35 30 25 20 15

6 12 18 24 30 36 42 48

6) How many 5 ¢ coins make up 55 ¢?

11 coins

7) A baker makes 3 cakes. He decorates each of them with 9 stars. How many stars does he make? Fill in the numbers.

3 cakes × 9 stars = 27 stars

8) How many petals are there on each bunch of flowers?

28 petals   25 petals   36 petals

These varied questions and activities help children develop an understanding of multiplication. If children are finding it difficult, encourage them to visually represent the question with circles, or provide them with beads, buttons, or counters.

14

Look at this graph to see how many loaves of bread a baker sells in a week.

= 10 loaves   = 5 loaves

Days of the Week	Number of Loaves Sold	Total Sold
Monday		45
Tuesday		50
Wednesday		55
Thursday		35
Friday		40
Saturday		65
Sunday		30

1) Fill in the total number of loaves sold for each day.

15

2) On which day did the baker sell the most loaves?
Saturday

3) How many loaves were sold in total on Monday and Tuesday?
95 loaves

4) How many more loaves were sold on Friday than Thursday?
5 loaves

5) How many loaves did the baker sell over the weekend?
95 loaves

6) How many loaves did the baker sell over the whole week?
320 loaves

7) The cost of 5 loaves is $2.50. How much did the baker make on Tuesday?
$25

8) On which day did he make $20 from selling the loaves?
Friday

Pictographs are a way of visually representing data. Make sure children note that a whole loaf equals 10 loaves and half a loaf equals 5 loaves before progressing with the questions.

Solving problems using the information presented in the pictograph may require one or two steps to calculate the answers.

Answers:

16–17 Dividing
18–19 Time Schedules

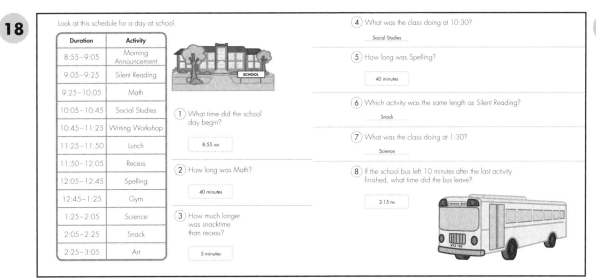

16

1. Share 28 candies equally among 4 children. How many candies did each child get? Fill in the numbers.

   28 candies ÷ 4 children = 7 candies

2. Join the questions to the answers with a line.

   Divide 20 by 4 — 9
   Divide 45 by 5 — 12
   Divide 77 by 7 — 5
   Divide 36 by 3 — 11

3. Sixty children were going on a school trip. They were split into 12 groups. How many children were there in each group? Fill in the numbers.

   60 children ÷ 12 groups = 5 children

4. How many groups of 4 are there in

   12? 3   32? 8   48? 12

17

5. Twenty-four cartons of milk are split equally among 3 classes. How many cartons of milk will each class get? Fill in the numbers.

   24 cartons ÷ 3 classes = 8 cartons

6. Fill in the missing numbers in each row.

   48 40 32 24 16 8   0
   63 54 45 36 27 18 9
   70 63 56 49 42 35 28

7. A restaurant is set up with 80 chairs split equally around 10 tables. How many chairs are there around each table?

   8 chairs

8. Complete the chart.

×	3	8
6	18	48
4	12	32

These questions and activities help children develop an understanding of division. Check that your child is aware of the relationship between multiplying and dividing, and that division involves sharing equally. Have a variety of objects on hand if your child needs to visually represent the questions to calculate the answers.

18

Look at this schedule for a day at school.

Duration	Activity
8:55–9:05	Morning Announcement
9:05–9:25	Silent Reading
9:25–10:05	Math
10:05–10:45	Social Studies
10:45–11:25	Writing Workshop
11:25–11:50	Lunch
11:50–12:05	Recess
12:05–12:45	Spelling
12:45–1:25	Gym
1:25–2:05	Science
2:05–2:25	Snack
2:25–3:05	Art

1. What time did the school day begin?

   8:55 AM

2. How long was Math?

   40 minutes

3. How much longer was snacktime than recess?

   5 minutes

19

4. What was the class doing at 10:30?

   Social Studies

5. How long was Spelling?

   40 minutes

6. Which activity was the same length as Silent Reading?

   Snack

7. What was the class doing at 1:30?

   Science

8. If the school bus left 10 minutes after the last activity finished, what time did the bus leave?

   3:15 PM

Children practice both reading time and calculating time problems when working from schedules. This school schedule demonstrates how children can apply their knowledge of time to everyday situations.

Answers:

22-23 Multiplying Fun
24-25 Tiling Areas

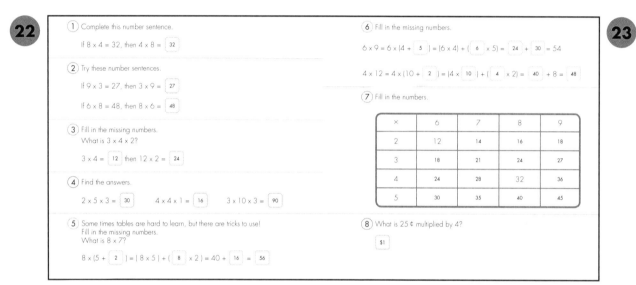

Children will begin to use strategies to multiply and divide as their understanding of properties develops. This page helps practice the commutative property in questions 1 and 2, the associative property in questions 3 and 4, and the distributive property in questions 5 and 6.

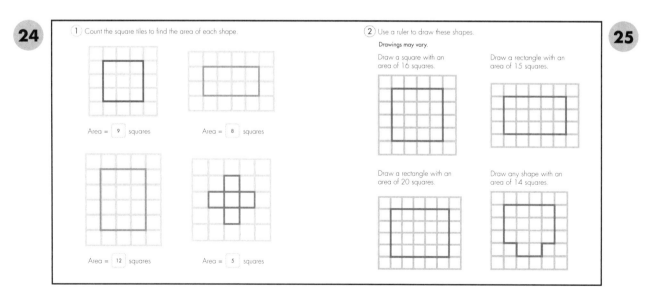

The concept of area is introduced through counting unit squares within a plane shape. This is related to the operations of multiplication and addition. Tiling is used to show that an area of a rectangle is calculated by multiplying the length by the width. Students will also learn that shapes can be split into non-overlapping rectangles and each area then added together to find the total area.

Answers:

26–27 Patterns
28–29 Volume of Liquids

26

1 Circle the odd numbers in this pattern.

(3)   6   (9)   12   (15)   18   (21)

2 Complete this pattern.

4   8   12   16   20   24

Are the answers odd or even?   Even

3 Fill in the missing numbers.

(+3)   45   48   51   54   57   60

(–3)   81   78   75   72   69   66

4 What is happening in these patterns?

30   36   42   48   54   60   6 is added

80   72   64   56   48   40   8 is subtracted

These patterns draw on knowledge of multiplication tables as children need to find the relationship between numbers. Multiples occur when two whole numbers are multiplied together.

27

5 This grid has numbers from 1 to 100.

1	2	3	4	5	6	7	8	9	10
11	12	13	14	15	16	17	18	19	20
21	22	23	24	25	26	27	28	29	30
31	32	33	34	35	36	37	38	39	40
41	42	43	44	45	46	47	48	49	50
51	52	53	54	55	56	57	58	59	60
61	62	63	64	65	66	67	68	69	70
71	72	73	74	75	76	77	78	79	80
81	82	83	84	85	86	87	88	89	90
91	92	93	94	95	96	97	98	99	100

Color all the multiples of 3 red.
Color all the multiples of 4 green.
Color all the multiples of 5 blue.

Which numbers are multiples of 3 and 5?	Which number is a multiple of 3, 4, and 5?
15 30 45 60 75 90	60

The completed grid helps to show a visual representation of the pattern and the relationship between the multiples of 3, 4, and 5 times tables.

28

1 If 2 cups = 1 pint, and 2 pints = 1 quart, how many cups are there in 1 quart?

4 cups

2 Carol bought 10 pints of juice. How many cups does this make?
Note: 2 cups = 1 pint.

20 cups

3 Twenty-four children each drank half a cup of milk at school. How many whole cups of milk did they drink?

12 cups

4 If 1 gallon = 8 pints, how many pints are there in a 4-gallon barrel that is full?

32 pints

5 How many milliliters are there in a 1-liter bottle of water?

1,000 ml

Provide children with plenty of practice measuring amounts, so they become familiar with visual representations of quantities. If they are having

29

6 How much water is there in the measuring cup? Measure in milliliters.

100 ml

7 Round these volumes to the nearest 10 ml.

65 ml   70 ml

346 ml   350 ml

673 ml   670 ml

8 Six children each drank 8 ml of juice. How much juice did they drink in total? Mark this on the measuring cup.

48 ml

difficulty, encourage children to represent the problem visually. For ex. by drawing cups and writing the quantities.

Answers:

30–31 Adding
32–33 Bar Graphs

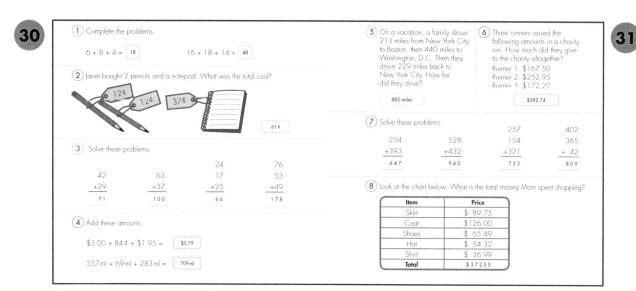

30

① Complete the problems.

$6 + 8 + 4 =$ 18 $16 + 18 + 14 =$ 48

② Janet bought 2 pencils and a notepad. What was the total cost?

12¢   12¢   37¢

61¢

③ Solve these problems.

		24	76
42	63	17	53
+29	+37	+25	+49
71	100	66	178

④ Add these amounts.

$3.00 + 84¢ + $1.95 =$ $5.79

$357\,ml + 69\,ml + 283\,ml =$ 709 ml

31

⑤ On a vacation, a family drove 213 miles from New York City to Boston, then 440 miles to Washington, D.C. Then they drove 229 miles back to New York City. How far did they drive?

882 miles

⑥ Three runners raised the following amounts in a charity run. How much did they give to the charity altogether?

Runner 1: $167.50
Runner 2: $252.95
Runner 3: $172.29

$592.74

⑦ Solve these problems.

254	528	257	402
		154	365
+393	+432	+321	+ 42
647	960	732	809

⑧ Look at the chart below. What is the total money Mom spent shopping?

Item	Price
Skirt	$ 89.75
Coat	$126.00
Shoes	$ 65.49
Hat	$ 54.32
Shirt	$ 36.99
Total	$ 3 7 2 . 5 5

Children should have a range of strategies for solving addition problems. For ex. being fluent with what numbers together make 10, carrying over in vertical addition, and using place value to add ones first, then tens, and then hundreds. Make sure they understand that for money problems, it is easier to calculate if all units are written out in the same format, for ex. 84¢ is $0.84.

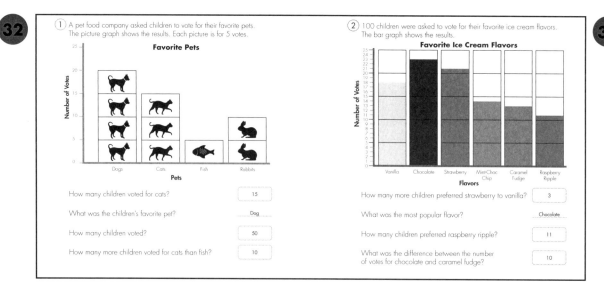

32

① A pet food company asked children to vote for their favorite pets. The picture graph shows the results. Each picture is for 5 votes.

Favorite Pets

How many children voted for cats?   15

What was the children's favorite pet?   Dog

How many children voted?   50

How many more children voted for cats than fish?   10

33

② 100 children were asked to vote for their favorite ice cream flavors. The bar graph shows the results.

Favorite Ice Cream Flavors

How many more children preferred strawberry to vanilla?   3

What was the most popular flavor?   Chocolate

How many children preferred raspberry ripple?   11

What was the difference between the number of votes for chocolate and caramel fudge?   10

Two different examples of graphs are shown here to demonstrate how each square or unit mark on the horizontal axis is a way of presenting information that can then be compared. Children should notice that each picture square stands for 5 votes for the pets graph, and they should be encouraged to use a ruler to align the top of the colored bar with the number of votes for the ice cream graph.

Answers:

34–35 Subtracting
36–37 Perimeters

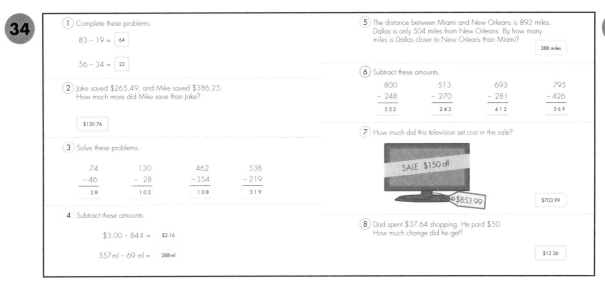

34

1. Complete these problems.

    $83 - 19 =$ 64

    $56 - 34 =$ 22

2. Jake saved $265.49, and Mike saved $386.25. How much more did Mike save than Jake?

    $120.76

3. Solve these problems.

74	130	462	538
− 46	− 28	− 354	− 219
28	102	108	319

4. Subtract these amounts.

    $3.00 − 84¢ = $2.16

    357 ml − 69 ml =   288 ml

35

5. The distance between Miami and New Orleans is 892 miles. Dallas is only 504 miles from New Orleans. By how many miles is Dallas closer to New Orleans than Miami?

    388 miles

6. Subtract these amounts.

800	513	693	795
− 248	− 270	− 281	− 426
552	243	412	369

7. How much did this television set cost in the sale?

    SALE $150 off $853.99 $703.99

8. Dad spent $37.64 shopping. He paid $50. How much change did he get?

    $12.36

Similar to addition, children should have a range of strategies for solving subtraction problems. Make sure that children understand that they are regrouping when there is not enough to take away from: they reduce by 1 and carry back or increase by 10.

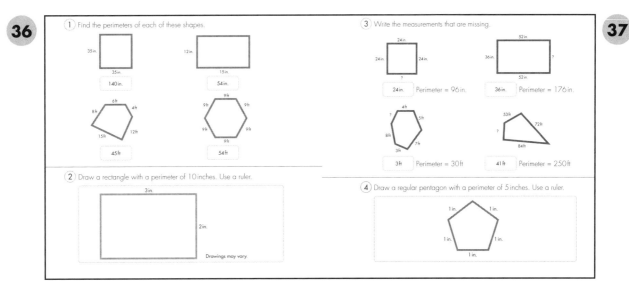

36

1. Find the perimeters of each of these shapes.

    35 in. / 35 in.   140 in.

    12 in. / 15 in.   54 in.

    6 ft / 8 ft / 4 ft / 15 ft / 12 ft   45 ft

    9 ft / 9 ft / 9 ft / 9 ft / 9 ft / 9 ft   54 ft

2. Draw a rectangle with a perimeter of 10 inches. Use a ruler.

    3 in. / 2 in.   Drawings may vary.

37

3. Write the measurements that are missing.

    24 in. / 24 in. / 24 in. / ?   24 in.   Perimeter = 96 in.

    52 in. / 36 in. / ? / 52 in.   36 in.   Perimeter = 176 in.

    4 ft / ? / 5 ft / 8 ft / 7 ft / 3 ft   3 ft   Perimeter = 30 ft

    53 ft / 72 ft / ? / 84 ft   41 ft   Perimeter = 250 ft

4. Draw a regular pentagon with a perimeter of 5 inches. Use a ruler.

    1 in. / 1 in. / 1 in. / 1 in. / 1 in.

Perimeter is the total sum of all the sides of a 2-D shape. Children are challenged to not only calculate perimeters by adding, but also find an unknown length by adding and subtracting. These pages also ask children to draw shapes with a given perimeter. There can be many answers, ex. for question 2, a rectangle could be drawn with two sides equal to 1 in. and the other two equal to 4 in.

Answers:

38–39 Solving Problems
42–43 Multiples of 10

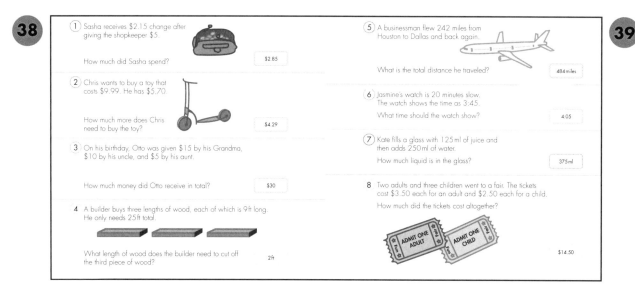

38

1) Sasha receives $2.15 change after giving the shopkeeper $5.

How much did Sasha spend? `$2.85`

2) Chris wants to buy a toy that costs $9.99. He has $5.70.

How much more does Chris need to buy the toy? `$4.29`

3) On his birthday, Otto was given $15 by his Grandma, $10 by his uncle, and $5 by his aunt.

How much money did Otto receive in total? `$30`

4 A builder buys three lengths of wood, each of which is 9 ft long. He only needs 25 ft total.

What length of wood does the builder need to cut off the third piece of wood? `2 ft`

39

5) A businessman flew 242 miles from Houston to Dallas and back again.

What is the total distance he traveled? `484 miles`

6) Jasmine's watch is 20 minutes slow. The watch shows the time as 3:45.

What time should the watch show? `4.05`

7) Kate fills a glass with 125 ml of juice and then adds 250 ml of water.

How much liquid is in the glass? `375 ml`

8 Two adults and three children went to a fair. The tickets cost $3.50 each for an adult and $2.50 each for a child.

How much did the tickets cost altogether? `$14.50`

Problem solving involves reading the question carefully, identifying the numbers to use, and deciding which of the four operations (+, −, x, ÷) is required. At this grade, the problems sometimes involve two steps. For ex. question 4 involves a first step to multiply and then a second step to subtract.

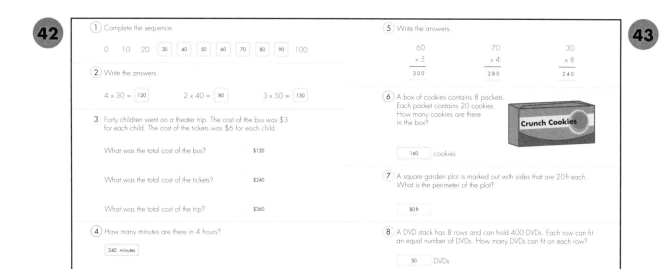

42

1) Complete the sequence.

0   10   20   `30`   `40`   `50`   `60`   `70`   `80`   `90`   100

2) Write the answers.

$4 \times 30 =$ `120` $2 \times 40 =$ `80` $3 \times 50 =$ `150`

3 Forty children went on a theater trip. The cost of the bus was $3 for each child. The cost of the tickets was $6 for each child.

What was the total cost of the bus? `$120`

What was the total cost of the tickets? `$240`

What was the total cost of the trip? `$360`

4) How many minutes are there in 4 hours?

`240` minutes

43

5) Write the answers.

| 60 | 70 | 30 |
x 5	x 4	x 8
300	280	240

6) A box of cookies contains 8 packets. Each packet contains 20 cookies. How many cookies are there in the box?

Crunch Cookies

`160` cookies

7) A square garden plot is marked out with sides that are 20 ft each. What is the perimeter of the plot?

`80 ft`

8 A DVD stack has 8 rows and can hold 400 DVDs. Each row can fit an equal number of DVDs. How many DVDs can fit on each row?

`50` DVDs

Multiplying one-digit numbers by multiples of 10 is the first step to more complex multiplication. A good understanding of place value will help as children multiply the single digit by 0 in the ones column and write a 0 in the ones answer column, and then multiply by the number in the tens column to complete the tens (and hundreds) column for the answer.

Answers:

44-45 Measuring Weight
46-47 Equations

44 **45**

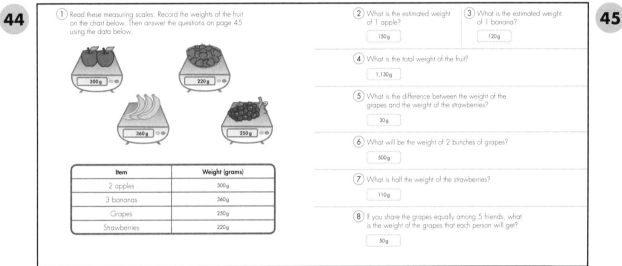

1. Read these measuring scales. Record the weights of the fruit on the chart below. Then answer the questions on page 45 using the data below.

Item	Weight (grams)
2 apples	300g
3 bananas	360g
Grapes	250g
Strawberries	220g

2. What is the estimated weight of 1 apple? **150g**
3. What is the estimated weight of 1 banana? **120g**
4. What is the total weight of the fruit? **1,130g**
5. What is the difference between the weight of the grapes and the weight of the strawberries? **30g**
6. What will be the weight of 2 bunches of grapes? **500g**
7. What is half the weight of the strawberries? **110g**
8. If you share the grapes equally among 5 friends, what is the weight of the grapes that each person will get? **50g**

Children will be introduced to the metric units of measurement for weights and mass of objects. Reading scales and estimating what weight an object may be are key skills in this topic. For solving the problems, encourage children to visually represent how they work out a solution.

46 **47**

1. What number is a?
$2 + a = 5$ **3** $a - 6 = 10$ **16**
$4 + a = 11$ **7** $8 - a = 3$ **5**
$a \times 10 = 120$ **12** $a \div 6 = 5$ **30**

2. Josh thinks of a number, takes 4 away from it, and adds 7. The answer is 13. What is the number Josh started with? **10**

3. I am four times bigger than 40. What number am I? **160**

4. What number is b?
$14 + 6 = 25 - b$ **5** $12 - 3 = 5 + b$ **4**
$36 \div 4 = 3 \times b$ **3** $2 \times 6 = 12 \times b$ **1**

5. Figure out each number on these teddy bears.
Double me to make 24. **12**
Take away 37 from 70 to get me. **33**
Add 3 to me to make 15. **12**
Subtract 19 from me to make 5. **24**
Multiply me by 6 to get 54. **9**
Divide me by 4 to get 7. **28**

Children need to understand the relationship between addition and subtraction, and also multiplication and division, to be able to find the unknown whole number in equations. An equation is when the value of one side equals the value of the other. Encourage children to check their answers by replacing the missing letter with their answer and checking what each side equals.

75

Answers:

48–49 Line Graph
50–51 Fractions of a Whole

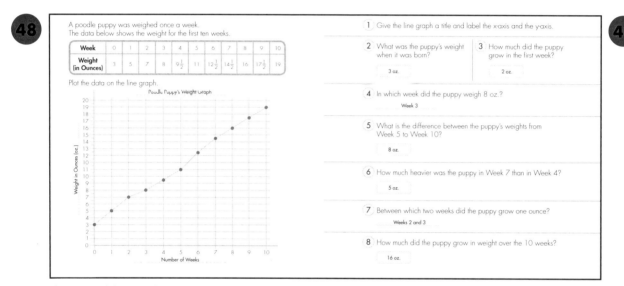

48

A poodle puppy was weighed once a week.
The data below shows the weight for the first ten weeks.

Week	0	1	2	3	4	5	6	7	8	9	10
Weight (in Ounces)	3	5	7	8	$9\frac{1}{2}$	11	$12\frac{1}{2}$	$14\frac{1}{2}$	16	$17\frac{1}{2}$	19

Plot the data on the line graph.

Poodle Puppy's Weight Graph

49

1. Give the line graph a title and label the x-axis and the y-axis.

2. What was the puppy's weight when it was born?
   3 oz.

3. How much did the puppy grow in the first week?
   2 oz.

4. In which week did the puppy weigh 8 oz.?
   Week 3

5. What is the difference between the puppy's weights from Week 5 to Week 10?
   8 oz.

6. How much heavier was the puppy in Week 7 than in Week 4?
   5 oz.

7. Between which two weeks did the puppy grow one ounce?
   Weeks 2 and 3

8. How much did the puppy grow in weight over the 10 weeks?
   16 oz.

Plotting and then analyzing growth measurements over time is one use of a line graph. Being able to plot the measurements by cross-checking between the values on the vertical and horizontal axes can be tricky. Encourage children to use a ruler to hold the position of one axis as they use their finger to find the position of the intercepting mark.

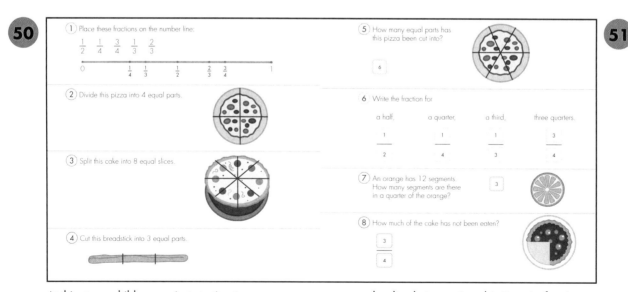

50

1. Place these fractions on the number line:
   $\frac{1}{2}$ $\frac{1}{4}$ $\frac{3}{4}$ $\frac{1}{3}$ $\frac{2}{3}$

2. Divide this pizza into 4 equal parts.

3. Split this cake into 8 equal slices.

4. Cut this breadstick into 3 equal parts.

51

5. How many equal parts has this pizza been cut into?
   6

6. Write the fraction for
   a half,   a quarter,   a third,   three quarters.
   $\frac{1}{2}$ $\frac{1}{4}$ $\frac{1}{3}$ $\frac{3}{4}$

7. An orange has 12 segments. How many segments are there in a quarter of the orange?
   3

8. How much of the cake has not been eaten?
   $\frac{3}{4}$

At this stage, children are just starting to understand the concept of fractions. They are given plenty of practice dividing a whole object into a certain number of equal parts, and also on a number line between 0 and 1. To write fractions, the number of equal parts of the whole goes on the bottom, called the denominator.

Answers:

52-53 Fractions of Shapes
54-55 Compare Fractions

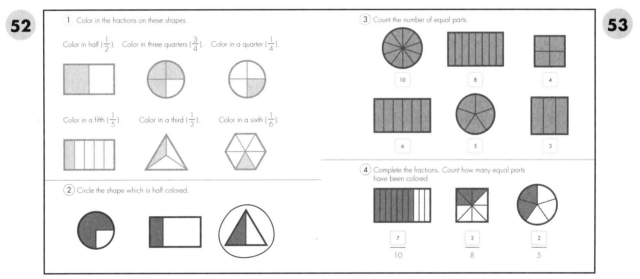

Children's understanding of fractions is further reinforced by partitioning shapes into parts with equal areas, and describing this as a fraction.

The top number of a fraction indicates the number of equal parts that need to be colored. This top number is called the numerator.

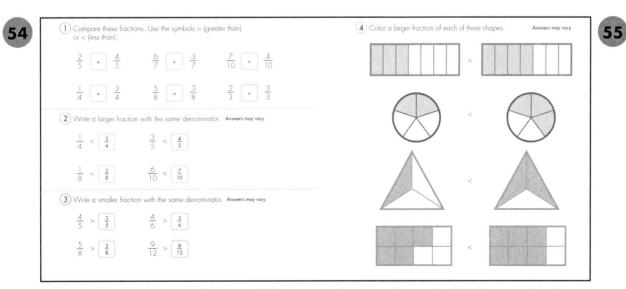

These pages practice comparing fractions with the same denominator. A larger fraction will have more equal parts of the whole, so the numerator will be greater. The > or < symbols always open up to the larger number. In school, children may have been taught that the "alligator mouth" will "eat" the bigger number to help them remember.

Answers:

56–57 Measuring Problems
58–59 Equivalent Fractions

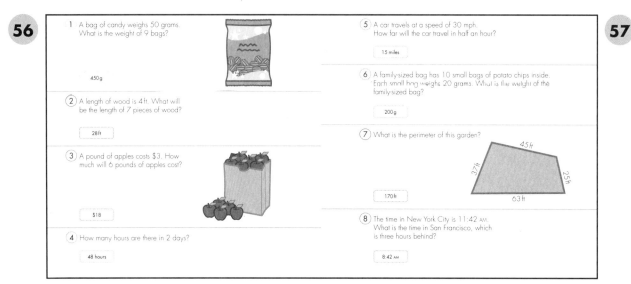

56

1 A bag of candy weighs 50 grams. What is the weight of 9 bags?

450g

2 A length of wood is 4 ft. What will be the length of 7 pieces of wood?

28 ft

3 A pound of apples costs $3. How much will 6 pounds of apples cost?

$18

4 How many hours are there in 2 days?

48 hours

57

5 A car travels at a speed of 30 mph. How far will the car travel in half an hour?

15 miles

6 A family-sized bag has 10 small bags of potato chips inside. Each small bag weighs 20 grams. What is the weight of the family-sized bag?

200g

7 What is the perimeter of this garden?

170 ft

45 ft 37 ft 25 ft 63 ft

8 The time in New York City is 11:42 AM. What is the time in San Francisco, which is three hours behind?

8:42 AM

Children should use the same logical approach to problem solving as on page 38 for these various measurement problems. While working out the operations, the units of measure can be dropped, but children should remember to include the unit of measure when they write the answer.

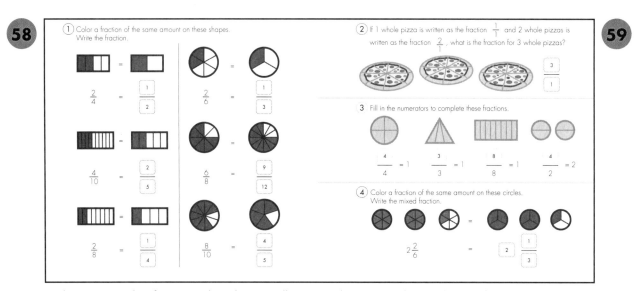

58

1 Color a fraction of the same amount on these shapes. Write the fraction.

$\frac{2}{4}$ = $\frac{1}{2}$ $\frac{2}{6}$ = $\frac{1}{3}$

$\frac{4}{10}$ = $\frac{2}{5}$ $\frac{6}{8}$ = $\frac{9}{12}$

$\frac{2}{8}$ = $\frac{1}{4}$ $\frac{8}{10}$ = $\frac{4}{5}$

59

2 If 1 whole pizza is written as the fraction $\frac{1}{1}$ and 2 whole pizzas is written as the fraction $\frac{2}{1}$, what is the fraction for 3 whole pizzas?

$\frac{3}{1}$

3 Fill in the numerators to complete these fractions.

$\frac{4}{4}$ = 1 $\frac{3}{3}$ = 1 $\frac{8}{8}$ = 1 $\frac{4}{2}$ = 2

4 Color a fraction of the same amount on these circles. Write the mixed fraction.

$2\frac{2}{6}$ = $2\frac{1}{3}$

Explaining equivalent fractions is best done visually. For question 1, children need to color the same amount on the shape and then write the fraction by counting the equal parts of the whole (denominator) and then how many parts have been colored (numerator).

Answers:

60–61 Areas
62–63 More Problems

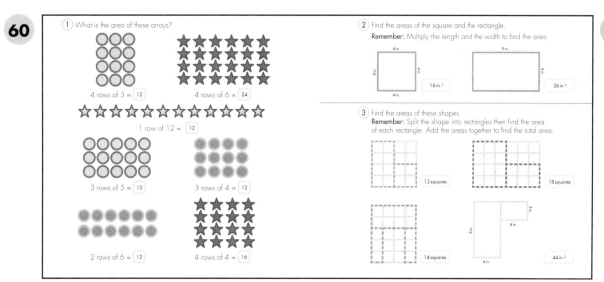

60

① What is the area of these arrays?

4 rows of 3 = 12   4 rows of 6 = 24

1 row of 12 = 12

3 rows of 5 = 15   3 rows of 4 = 12

2 rows of 6 = 12   4 rows of 4 = 16

61

② Find the areas of the square and the rectangle.
Remember: Multiply the length and the width to find the area.

4 in.   9 in.

4 in.   4 in.

16 in.²   36 in.²

③ Find the areas of these shapes.
Remember: Split the shape into rectangles then find the area of each rectangle. Add the areas together to find the total area.

12 squares   18 squares

14 squares   3 in. 4 in. 8 in. 4 in. 44 in.²

Arrays are visual diagrams of multiplication problems. They help children count the number of rows and the number of columns, and then multiply the numbers. This concept of multiplying width and height is transferred to calculating areas of squares and rectangles. For the irregular shapes, encourage children to first split the shape into rectangles.

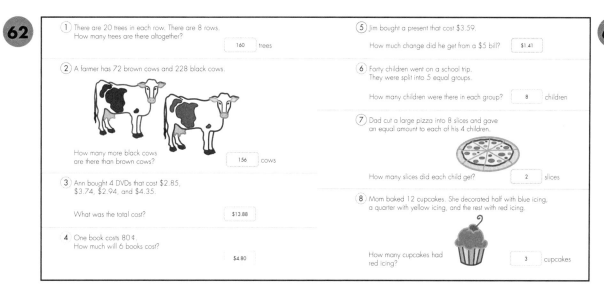

62

① There are 20 trees in each row. There are 8 rows. How many trees are there altogether?
160 trees

② A farmer has 72 brown cows and 228 black cows.
How many more black cows are there than brown cows?
156 cows

③ Ann bought 4 DVDs that cost $2.85, $3.74, $2.94, and $4.35.
What was the total cost?
$13.88

④ One book costs 80¢.
How much will 6 books cost?
$4.80

63

⑤ Jim bought a present that cost $3.59.
How much change did he get from a $5 bill?
$1.41

⑥ Forty children went on a school trip. They were split into 5 equal groups.
How many children were there in each group?
8 children

⑦ Dad cut a large pizza into 8 slices and gave an equal amount to each of his 4 children.
How many slices did each child get?
2 slices

⑧ Mom baked 12 cupcakes. She decorated half with blue icing, a quarter with yellow icing, and the rest with red icing.
How many cupcakes had red icing?
3 cupcakes

These word problems provide extra practice in applying the four operations and fractions. Encourage children to show their work in the space available so that you can see if and where an error is made. Children can also visually draw the fraction problems if necessary. Whenever an opportunity arises, provide children with math problems to solve in daily life, perhaps when shopping, or preparing and serving meals.

Answers:

20–21 Beat the Clock 1
40–41 Beat the Clock 2
64–65 Beat the Clock 3

These pages test your child's mental math skills. Although these questions are answered against the clock, make sure that children do not feel pressured to rush their answers. It is more important to be accurate.

They can come back to try again and beat the clock at another time. You may want to keep a record of the time taken and score on each try.

20–21

#		#		#		#		#		#	
1	100	2	80	3	14	31	28	32	24	33	60
4	4	5	0	6	30	34	12	35	27	36	48
7	9	8	90	9	12	37	72	38	42	39	70
10	16	11	24	12	7	40	0	41	18	42	55
13	25	14	22	15	6	43	36	44	48	45	66
16	36	17	44	18	20	46	35	47	8	48	30
19	49	20	60	21	32	49	5	50	15	51	45
22	64	23	12	24	18	52	27	53	40	54	40
25	81	26	50	27	18	55	16	56	21	57	72
28	0	29	33	30	9	58	24	59	45	60	36

40–41

#		#		#		#		#		#	
1	21	2	25	3	15	31	7	32	37	33	72
4	20	5	33	6	17	34	3	35	38	36	26
7	31	8	24	9	19	37	8	38	86	39	37
10	37	11	33	12	13	40	46	41	56	42	8
13	29	14	27	15	16	43	4	44	18	45	73
16	75	17	56	18	19	46	9	47	25	48	18
19	80	20	46	21	12	49	19	50	27	51	33
22	72	23	38	24	19	52	5	53	19	54	62
25	82	26	46	27	16	55	25	56	21	57	69
28	118	29	63	30	14	58	8	59	37	60	66

64–65

#		#		#		#		#		#	
1	15	2	121	3	8	31	38	32	7	33	27
4	12	5	244	6	5	34	49	35	6	36	30
7	14	8	203	9	0	37	72	38	4	39	28
10	13	11	531	12	18	40	40	41	8	42	60
13	18	14	512	15	21	43	90	44	5	45	80
16	9	17	121	18	21	46	35	47	7	48	6
19	6	20	16	21	24	49	32	50	4	51	4
22	6	23	46	24	36	52	32	53	8	54	5
25	5	26	70	27	20	55	38	56	6	57	12
28	8	29	72	30	8	58	29	59	9	60	20